FACT PLANET

SETTLEMENTS

IZZI HOWELL

FRANKLIN WATTS
LONDON • SYDNEY

Franklin Watts
First published in Great Britain in 2020 by the Watts Publishing Group
Copyright © the Watts Publishing Group 2020

Produced for Franklin Watts by
White-Thomson Publishing Ltd
www.wtpub.co.uk

Series Editor: Izzi Howell
Designer: Clare Nicholas
Series Designer: Rocket Design (East Anglia) Ltd

HB ISBN: 978 1 4451 7275 0
PB ISBN: 978 1 4451 7276 7

All **bold** words appear in the glossary on page 30.

Getty: Tzviatko Chiderov 5t, chictype 7br and 28c, csfotoimages 16t, skeeg 18t, Guang Niu 20t, peeterv 25b, Huapu Zhao 27t and 29b; Shutterstock: VitaliyVill, Design tech art and ActiveLines cover, Artram title page and 4t, keko-ka 2 and 13bl, ProStockStudio 3 and 19b, Macrovector and Tartila 4b, Olena Tur 5c, vitalez 5b and 28t, ActiveLines 6t, vectorism7788 6b, turtix 7t, Blue Planet Studio 7bl, Lemberg Vector studio 8t and 17t, Faber14 8b, Stanislav71 9t, Travel mania 9b, CastecoDesign 10, Jon_Clark 11t, Korrapon Karapan 11b, elenabsl 12t, Viacheslav Lopatin 12b, Roschetzky Photography 13t, Trong Nguyen 13br and 28b, Thomas La Mela 14t, Iconic Bestiary 14b, Anna Sprenne 15t, Tupungato 15b, 17br and 29t, tarubumi, Faber14 and VectorsMarket 16b, Alexander Chaikin 17bl, Dino Geromella 18b, Photostravellers 19t, Antonio Salaverry 19c, rodnikovay 20b and 32, Ohishiapply 21t, Amit kg 21c, Hung Chung Chih 21b and 29cl, Igogosha 22t, GoodStudio 22b, Suriel Ramzal 23t, anna.q 23c, Fotos593 23b and 29cr, Sean Pavone 24t, Sky and glass 24b, elenabsl 25t, Marcin Osman 26t, SaveJungle 26b, matrioshka 27c and 30–31, polarman 27b.

Printed in Dubai

MIX
Paper from
responsible sources
FSC
www.fsc.org
FSC® C104740

Franklin Watts
An imprint of
Hachette Children's Group
Part of the Watts Publishing Group
Carmelite House
50 Victoria Embankment
London EC4Y 0DZ

An Hachette UK Company
www.hachette.co.uk
www.franklinwatts.co.uk

Find the answers to all questions in this book on page 28.

Contents

What is a settlement?

A settlement is a place where people live.

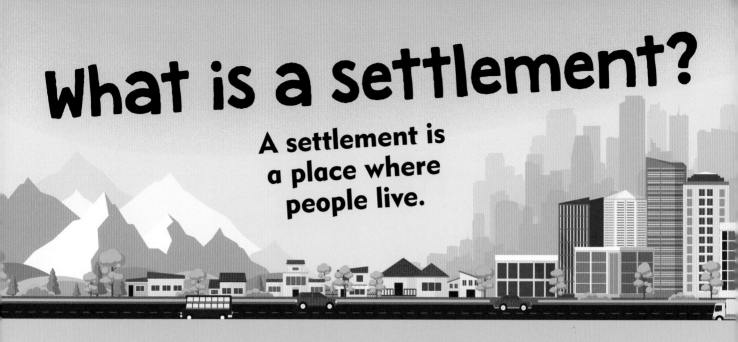

There are many different sizes of settlement. Some are tiny villages with just a few **residents**, while others are huge cities that are home to many thousands, or even millions, of people.

In the past, most people lived in small **rural** settlements and worked on farms. This changed with the arrival of factories and machines in the eighteenth **century** (1701–1799). Towns and cities grew around the new factories and people moved there to work. Over time, the **population** of these settlements grew bigger.

People have been living in the city of Plovdiv, Bulgaria, for over **8,000 years,** making it one of the oldest cities in the world!

Settlements often look different around the world. Buildings are made from various materials and in many styles. This often depends on the **climate** and location of the settlement. Some settlements have old buildings, while others are very modern.

Clay buildings in a town in the mountains of Morocco, Africa.

PICTURE PUZZLE

Which materials are the walls and the roof of this house made from?

Types of settlement

Settlements come in many sizes.

The smallest settlements are **hamlets** and villages. They are home to anywhere from a few people to several hundreds. These settlements are mainly made up of houses, with a few **facilities**, such as shops, restaurants and schools.

Towns are larger than villages. They have more facilities, which are used by the thousands of people who live there. There are many places for people to work and have fun.

New York
City, USA

Millions of people live in the biggest settlements on Earth – cities. They are so large that they are split into lots of smaller areas for shopping, businesses or homes (see pages 12–13).

The largest cities, with populations of over 10 million people, are known as **megacities**.

FACT!

Tokyo, Japan, has the largest population of any megacity. Over

37 million

people live there (see page 24).

PICTURE PUZZLE

This method of transport is often used in big cities. What is it?

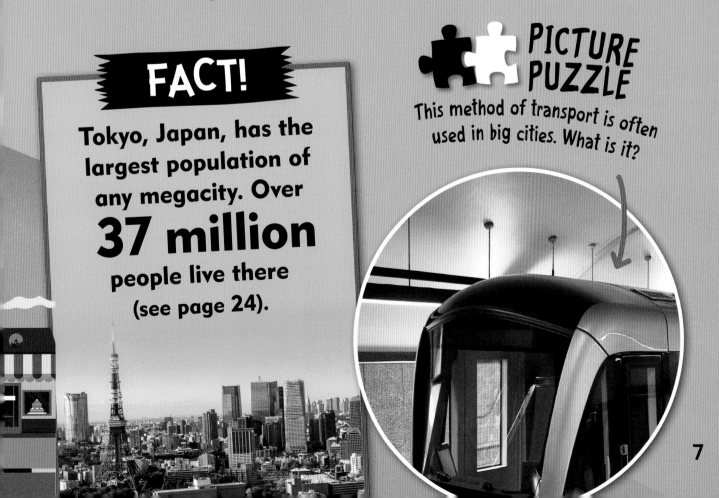

Settlement sites

People build settlements in sites with certain features.

When choosing a site for a new settlement, people look for large, open areas, which are easier to build on. Dry land is easier to build on, as the buildings won't sink into the ground.

QUESTION TIME

WHY WERE ANCIENT SETTLEMENTS OFTEN BUILT ON HILLS?

a People liked the fresh air up high

b People could see **invaders** coming and so it was easier to defend the settlement

c People thought it was good luck

Resources in the local area are also important. A settlement needs to be near places for farms to grow food, building materials, such as wood and stone, and clean drinking water.

FACT!

In some settlements with little freshwater, they remove the salt from sea water and use it for drinking and for watering plants.

A factory for removing salt from sea water in Dubai.

Settlements need to be connected to other settlements for **trade** and jobs. In the past, many settlements were built near rivers so that they could use boats as transport to carry goods and people to other places. Today, it's important for settlements to be close to roads and railways.

Objects are taken by ship from this city's port to other settlements.

Settlement shapes

Small villages and towns form in different shapes.

In some settlements, buildings are spread out over a large area. This is known as a dispersed settlement. They are often found in mountains, where it's hard to build houses on steep slopes, or in the countryside, where there are lots of farmhouses surrounded by fields.

In a nucleated settlement, buildings are packed closely together in one area. These settlements often grow around an important point, such as a bridge across a river, a place of worship, a castle or a train station.

church (place of worship)

In linear settlements, buildings are built in a long line. They often form along roads, rivers or narrow valleys where it is hard to build higher up the slopes.

QUESTION TIME

WHICH SETTLEMENT PATTERN IS MOST LIKELY ALONG THE BANKS OF A CANAL?

a Linear

b Dispersed

c Nucleated

Parts of a settlement

Large settlements can be divided into different areas with different features.

In the city centre, there are offices and shops. The city centre is often the oldest part of the city and may contain some old buildings. Over time, the settlement grew outwards from the centre.

FACT!

The Colosseum in the city centre of Rome, Italy, is nearly **2,000 years old!** It was built by the ancient Romans.

Suburbs are residential areas found towards the edges of towns and cities. There is more space in this area, so people often live in houses instead of flats.

There is lots of space on the outskirts of a settlement. Large buildings, such as big supermarkets and shops and **industrial** areas with warehouses and factories are built on the outskirts so that they have plenty of room.

PICTURE PUZZLE

What is this place that can usually be found in any part of a settlement – city centre, suburbs or outskirts?

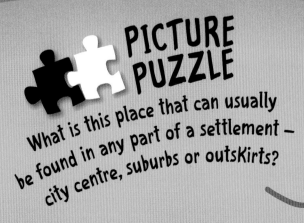

Settlement density

The number of people who live per area in a settlement is known as its **density**.

When many people live in a small area, we say that it has a high population density. Areas with a low population density are home to a lower number of people.

Cities often have higher population densities than smaller settlements. In a city, the highest density is usually in the centre. The density gets smaller as you move out towards the suburbs, where fewer people live in a larger area with more space.

Settlements with a high population density can have problems. There may be too many people for services such as public transport, healthcare and education. People may be forced to live in small, crowded houses as there isn't enough room for everyone.

FACT!

Manila, the capital city of the Philippines, is one of the most densely populated cities in the world with over **42,000 people** per square km.

In some places with high population density, people can end up living in poor-quality housing, as there are not enough homes to go around.

QUESTION TIME

WHICH OF THESE DOES NOT MAKE POPULATION DENSITY HIGHER?

a People adopting pets

b People moving to an area

c More babies being born in an area

Facilities

The larger the settlement, the more facilities it has.

Some settlements are so small that they don't have any facilities – only homes. Other small settlements have shops, cafes, a school or a doctor's surgery.

This village shop sells fruit and vegetables.

Towns have more facilities, including police stations, fire stations and larger schools. They usually have public transport links, such as railways and buses to other places.

POLICE

POLICE

Large cities have many facilities. The same facilities are built in many places across the city so that they can be used by people who live in different neighbourhoods. Facilities that are usually only found in big cities include large hospitals, universities and airports.

PICTURE PUZZLE

This type of building is found in many small and large settlements. What is it?

Homes

Homes are different in small villages and large cities.

In small settlements, there is often more space to build larger homes so people live in houses. These houses can be joined together or detached (separate).

Homes often look different around the world. People build homes from local materials, such as wood, bamboo or stone. In cold places, homes are designed to keep people warm, while in hot places, they are designed to be cool inside.

Cool air enters this house in Laos through the woven bamboo walls and big openings.

These houses in Iceland have thick walls made from wood and stone, and grass on the roofs to keep heat inside the building.

The Edifício Copan in São Paulo, Brazil, is one of the largest apartment blocks in the world, with

1,160 flats

inside!

In large towns and cities, space for homes is often an issue. Lots of homes need to be built in a small area. The solution is to build upwards, creating blocks of flats with lots of homes on top of each other.

Problems in settlements

Settlements of different sizes have different issues.

There are fewer jobs in small settlements so people can find it hard to make enough money to survive. Some have to travel a long way to find work. There are also fewer facilities so residents have to travel a long way to see a doctor, go to school or go to the supermarket.

These children in rural China have to walk for several hours through the mountains to get to school.

Cities often have higher rates of crime than smaller villages and towns. There are so many people that residents often don't know their neighbours. Some people living in cities can feel lonely.

There are often environmental problems in large cities. Traffic exhaust and factories create air pollution. There is also noise pollution from streets and businesses, and light pollution from street lights and buildings. Some cities have lots of rubbish on the street.

FACT!

22 of the 30 most polluted cities in the world are in India.

PICTURE PUZZLE

This boy is wearing something to protect him from air pollution. What is it?

changing settlements

Settlements change over time.

In the past few hundred years, many people have moved from the countryside to cities. This has made cities grow much larger. Over half of people around the world now live in **urban** areas.

In the next 50 years, the world population is expected to get much bigger. Many of these people will live in cities. This will create more problems in cities, such as overcrowding on public transport and pollution.

By the year 2050, **two thirds** of the world population are expected to live in cities.

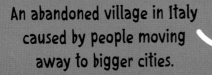

Mexico City

Sometimes, settlements can get smaller and even disappear! These are known as ghost towns. This often happens when new cities are built near natural resources. When the resources run out, people leave the city. There are many ghost cities in China. Villages are also abandoned when all the residents move to cities.

An abandoned village in Italy caused by people moving away to bigger cities.

PICTURE PUZZLE

Ghost towns can also be created when people leave because of a natural disaster. Which disaster can be seen here?

Megacities

These are some of the largest settlements in the world.

Tokyo is the largest megacity on Earth by population and the capital of Japan. Its population of 37 million includes people who live in the city itself, as well as smaller nearby towns and cities that are connected to Tokyo. Only around 9 million people live in the city of Tokyo itself.

Crowds of people in the megacity of Tokyo, Japan.

New York City, USA, is the largest megacity by land area, measuring over 7,300 square km. As with Tokyo, New York City also includes many towns and cities in the surrounding area across four different US states. Over 20 million people live in this megacity, attracted by jobs in finance, trade and entertainment.

There many other huge megacities around the world. Some of the largest cities in Asia are the megacities of Shanghai and Beijing in China, and Mumbai and Delhi in India. Outside of Asia, there are massive megacities such as Lagos in Nigeria, Mexico City in Mexico and Cairo in Egypt.

FACT!

Experts think that by 2100, Lagos could be the biggest city in the world with

88 million

residents!

QUESTION TIME

WHICH OF THESE MEGACITIES IS IN SOUTH AMERICA?

a Bangkok

 **b** Seoul

 Rio de Janeiro

Extreme settlements

Some settlements are built in places where it is hard to live.

La Rinconada in Peru is the highest settlement in the world at 5,100 m above sea level. It is home to around 50,000 people. Most residents work in a gold mine that the town is built around. There are no sewers or running water because of the height.

Tristan da Cunha is a group of islands in the south Atlantic Ocean where the most remote settlements in the world can be found. There are no airports on the island. The only way to reach the settlements is by boat, which takes seven days from South Africa. If people need to go to hospital urgently, they are taken to South Africa on passing fishing boats.

PICTURE PUZZLE

Many species of bird are found on Tristan da Cunha, including this one. What is it?

Small settlements have been built on Antarctica, which is one of the coldest places on Earth. Scientists live there while they research the weather, animals and rocks in the area. Most scientists only stay during summer when the weather is less **extreme**.

FACT!

Scientists living in Antarctica have to deal with temperatures ranging from –10 °C to –60 °C!

Answers

PAGE 5

Picture Puzzle:
The walls are made from wood and the roof is made from straw

PAGE 7

Picture Puzzle:
An underground train

PAGE 8

Question Time!
b) People could see invaders coming and so it was easier to defend the settlement

PAGE 11

Question Time! a) Linear

PAGE 13

Picture Puzzle: A park

Glossary

century a period of one hundred years

climate the normal weather in an area

density the number of people in an area compared to the size of the place

extreme very serious or unusual

facility a place where a particular activity happens

hamlet a small village

industrial related to factories

invader someone who uses force to try to take over an area

megacity a large city with a population of over 10 million people

population the number of people (or animals) living in an area, or on Earth

resident someone who lives in an area

resource a natural material used to make something

rural related to the countryside

trade buying or selling goods

urban related to cities

Further information

Books

Mapping a City by Jen Green (Wayland, 2016)

Population and Settlement (Geographics) by Izzi Howell
(Franklin Watts, 2018)

Settlements (World Feature Focus) by Rebecca Kahn
(Franklin Watts, 2020)

Websites

www.bbc.co.uk/bitesize/topics/zx72pv4/articles/zrbvjhv
Learn more about settlements and test your knowledge with a quiz.

www.nationalgeographic.org/interactive/age-megacities/
Explore an interactive infographic about megacities.

www.worldatlas.com/articles/15-traditional-house-types-from-around-the-world.html
Look at some traditional houses from around the world.

Index

More titles in the the **Fact Planet** series

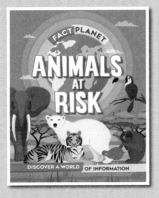

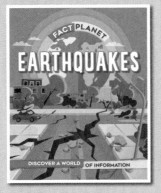
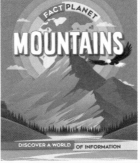

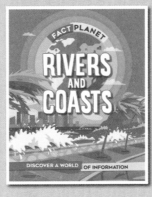